BENEATH ROSE-LEMON SKIES

BENEATH ROSE-LEMON SKIES
Contemporary Light Verse

Keith and Elizabeth Stanley-Mallett

ARTHUR H. STOCKWELL LTD
Torrs Park   Ilfracombe   Devon
Established 1898
www.ahstockwell.co.uk

© *Keith & Elizabeth Stanley-Mallett, 2009*
First published in Great Britain, 2009
All rights reserved.
*No part of this publication may be reproduced
or transmitted in any form or by any means,
electronic or mechanical, including photocopy,
recording, or any information storage and
retrieval system, without permission
in writing from the copyright holder.*

*British Library Cataloguing-in-Publication Data.
A catalogue record for this book is available
from the British Library.*

Previously published poems by the same author:
Conspiracy of Faculties – Poetry Now, 1994
Yielding Forms – Poetry Now, 1994
One, That are We – Poetry Now, 1994
Two Minutes of Silence – Anchor Books, 1994
A Norfolk Winter Sunset – Poets England Series, Brentham Press, 1994
Come Silently to Me – Poetry Now, 1995
To the Eye – Poetry Now, 1995
World Wide Conceded Nationally – Poetry Now, 1996
Three Times Twenty – Poetry Now, 1996
I Believe in Betjeman – Poetry Now, 1996
Emotive Machine – Poetry Now, 1996
Essence of Time – Poetry Now, 1996
Poetic Visions – Poetry Now, 1996
Once Upon a Time – Poetry Now, 1996
The Red Fox – Anchor Books, 1997
Soul Winds – Poetry Now, 1997
Across a Timeless Threshold – Anchor Books, 1999
Mrs Batholomew's Door – Anchor Books, 1999
Electronic Life – United Press, 1999
Under An Indigo Moon – Arthur H. Stockwell Ltd, 2009

ISBN 978-0-7223-3976-3 Paperback edition.
ISBN 978-0-7223-3975-6 Cloth-bound edition.
*Printed in Great Britain by
Arthur H. Stockwell Ltd
Torrs Park   Ilfracombe
Devon*

FOREWORD

BOOK I

Poems by
Keith Stanley-Mallett

The poems in Book I by the above author were written as a hoped-for later sequel to the recently published *Under An Indigo Moon*, published by Arthur H Stockwell Ltd.

They are here reproduced in a shared sequel with work by his wife, Elizabeth, in this volume *Beneath Rose-Lemon Skies*. These poems reflect a subtle change of style in his work.

Writing since 1959, he has tried to bring colour and simplicity to his work; believing that poetry should be easily read. Distilled to a point but communicative as a priority.

BOOK II

Poems by
Elizabeth Stanley-Mallett

The following poems in Book II by Elizabeth Stanley-Mallett are her first works to be published. These reflect her attitude, and her emotional need, to understand life. Her interpretations of subject are clear and uncluttered.

All poems in Book I and Book II are original and previously unpublished.

BOOK I

PRESENTED LIGHT VERSE

By

Keith Stanley-Mallett

CONTENTS

Book I – 2008

The Gods That Ruled Are The Gods That Lied	13
Enough	14
Innocence Lost	15
Little Thoughts	16
Rural Aspect	17
The Hourglass	18
An Embrace	19
Asleep	20
And Is It True?	21
The Very Atmosphere	22
Into Twilight Skies	23
Ode to Young Dreams	24
Into the Twenty-First Century	25
Fronds of Willow	26
Tell Me Now	27
Winter Elements	28
The Tale-Teller	29
No More Will I Ride the Highway	30
Living Marionettes	31
By Track and Muddied Lane	32
So It Ever Will Be	33
One Step Further	34
Mist	35
Why Do You Ask?	36
Winter Contrives	37
All Is White	38
Gravity	39
Locomotive	40
Day Progresses	41
Among the Crowd	42
Burning Flame	43
The Tree	44
A Silver Sun	45
Due Care	46
Clocks	47
'Tis Not Just the Light	48

Rose-Lemon Skies	49
Sundown	50
Forgotten House	51
The Biggest Game of All	52
Dogs	53
The Days of Old England	54
Fiction to Future Days	55
Degree by Degree	56
Intrigue and Greed	57
Ignition	58
Foolish Fancies and Other	59
A Ship of Shadows	60
The Printed Word	62
In My Mind	63
The Rainbow	64
Meteor	65
Old Secrets	66
Christmas Morning	67
Between Dawn and Twilight	68
True Pie or Fable	69
A Winter View of an English Village	70
Life	71
Nothing Is Carved in Stone	73
Old Year, Old Lore	74
Eleven or Even Twenty-Six	75
A Godlike Style	76
A Single Sunbeam	77
My Country	78
We, Free Men	79
Children of the Mind	80
Two Cats and a Dog	81
So Short a Time	82
Earth's Historic Song	83
The Haunting Song	84
Winter Rain	85
Quietly She Will Sleep	86
In Brilliant Splendour	87
Wimblington Village	88
From Your Doorstep	89
Sentimental Journeys	90

Of Meadows Sweet	91
Middling, Muddling, Maudlin	92
Procession	93
Thoughts on Destructive Construction	94
A One-Time Suburbia	95
Ten Million Sparkling Stars	96
Garden Goblin	97
Upon a Skyline	98
A Thunderbird	99
On Wind Power	100
Nature's Bath Day	101
Nature's Heyday	102
Nature's Clean Day	103
Progression To Regression Via TV	104
From Here To Where?	105
Beyond the Yonder	107
The Creator and the Destroyer	108
Fall of Night	109
Winter Elementals	110
Snow	111
Particles of Everything	112
The Prize Is Yours	113
Impedimenta Regimen-ta	114
The Coming of Spring	115
Time and the Hour	116
Rabbits All	117
Universe of One	118
The Eternal Habitat	119
A Blue Chevrolet	120
An English Lane	121
The Colour of Light	122
Dracula's Daughter	123
Life Extraordinaire	124
Rest the Pen?	125

The Gods That Ruled Are The Gods That Lied

Aeon upon aeon, came each star sign.
   Five hundred thousand years of yore,
Incomprehensible passing of time
   Highlighted by pyramids built to soar.

Wrought upon us by desperate Gods
   Long-lived, harbouring their flaws in men,
Adam, created, programmed, naked, unshod.
   Beginnings of men in likeness to them.

Gods who ruled with bribery and fear,
   Changing our image to what they required.
Twisting truth to the primitive ear,
   Moulding the newborn recently sired.

Such Gods that ruled were the Gods that lied.
   Their reasons were not so benign in plan,
They ruled with jealousy, fought and tried
   The earth to tame, forgetting THERE STOOD MAN.

Enough

I thought I'd written enough
   About age, during past years,
Writing throughout a lifetime
   With happiness and tears.

I thought I had seen enough
   Of places far and wide,
Remembering old times,
   The town, village, coast and tide.

I thought I had heard enough
   Of worldly news events,
Constant evil, famine, war,
   Mediocrity content.

I thought I'd written enough
   About humanity's state,
Yet how can I still refrain,
   For writing cannot wait.

Innocence Lost

From the conception of man
   Down those long-lost thousands of years.
The time of Sumer and Ur
   The forgotten struggles and fears.

Newborn were in innocence
   Unknowing the secret powers.
That commanded and ruled,
   While building the mighty towers.

Through time to the present day
   Accustomed to tradition.
Festivals, Christmas and Easter,
   Teaching, prayer, all renditions.

Of worship and glory given
   To mystical people unbound.
Primitive man was driven
   By Godlike beings profound.

Then today I understood
   The teachings heard as a child,
Now decoded tablets reveal
   The truth we were beguiled.

I knew then man had passed
   From innocence to knowing mind,
Others like me knew the Gods
   Had run their ancient course sublime.

Along with this new century
   Come ever new ideas.
Technical innovations go
   In hand, with reasons thinking, clear.

Little Thoughts

There's a squirrel just next door.
    He lives in a green fir tree.
When he thinks I'm not about
    He capers most craftily.

Running along the fence tops,
    Or rummaging in the grass,
Flicking his tail jauntily
    When he finds a nut at last.

Then sitting upon a post,
    So quiet, still and feral.
I wonder, are you thinking
    Little thoughts, Little Squirrel.

Rural Aspect

There's a meadow or two I can see
    Across from this cottage window.
While leaves of distant trees and shrubs,
    In the autumn sun do brightly glow.

A picture set, now and as before,
    Part of England's tranquillity.
Watching the sheep and ponies graze
    In natural calm pacivity.

Beyond, in the lea of sheltering trees,
    Chicken coops, with birds running free.
Beside the hedgerows mingling
    In the fields, with rabbits wild to see.

Feather-soft clouds drift to horizons
    Making the scene quite perfect.
As from this cottage window view
    A typical rural aspect.

The Hourglass

The hourglass stands upon the desk,
    Sand and glass reflecting time
Within the ornate frame of brass,
    Made exception, craft and line.

Thus a tool of passing hours
    Limiting each labour's task,
Or multiplying that to serve
    Such work or pastime, to last.

Yet, there I see an ornament
    In style and beauty engendered.
Still, it needs the hand of man
    To count the hours, by turn rendered.

An Embrace

Equal to, yet more than
    Your lover's soft embrace,
The morning, born brightly
    New, fresh of golden face.

Beguiling the spirit,
    In summer's warmth enfold.
Crystal dew underfoot
    Minute reflections hold.

Trees with blossoms hanging
    Heavy in nature's scent,
A loving soft embrace
    Equal, in pleasure meant.

Asleep

To sleep is but a shallow death
    Born of fatigue and necessity,
To sleep is but to leave for rest
    All consciousness and reality.

To drift unconscious and alone
    To where time itself stands still.
For the inner mind, dreams, to roam,
    For you are all, existence fill'd.

And thus in stasis lost for thought,
    While drifting endless, remaining,
Unthinking and uncaring, brought
    Back to life, by nature's waking.

And Is It True?

And is it true, those ancients knew
    When history would cease.
That comes a time, a day, when all
    The living world's deceased.

For those ancient, scattered writings
    Have come to life of late.
Correlating codes, signs and myth
    Slowly to knowledge, relate.

And are we in the last of years
    As stated long ago.
One Godlike being, long before
    Humanity began to know –

With a greater philosophy
    Spoke, his words to transcend,
The end is the beginning
    The beginning is the end.

The Very Atmosphere

Although I love my country
    It has become most drear,
And it's not just the weather
    But the very atmosphere.

If it wasn't bad enough
    November's mist and rain,
So dreary, damp, dark and cold
    No wonder we complain.

We have as well taxation,
    More than our share should be,
Crippling all the small folk,
    Demanded, greedily.

Introducing petty laws
    In thousands, are numbered,
Are they so miserable
    Freedom must be plundered.

Although I love my country,
    It has become most drear,
For it's more than the weather
    It's the very atmosphere.

Into Twilight Skies

See the lamps a-twinkling
    Early in the eve,
See the sun a-sinking
    Fire-bright to perceive.

Now the clouds a-drifting
    Low, to dim-lit views,
While bats start a-lifting
    To night's veiled hues.

Then the moon a-rising
    Into twilight skies,
Her silver a-shining
    As golden light dies.

Ode to Young Dreams

Yesterday, as a child at school,
    As young as a newborn day,
Laughter and mischief uppermost
    In a mind unsullied and gay.

Then growing to maturity
    Amidst the world's loud tumult,
Did you seek for those childish dreams
    Or yearn to be an adult.

Oh, did you wish so earnestly
    For things, to be different,
When you thought the world would change
    With adventure, so imminent.

Slowly, did you realise
    As mind and heart matured,
That the world is not a plaything
    And to dreams, become inured.

Into the Twenty First-Century

Although still quite early
In this twenty-first century,
Life is being catalogued,
Reads like an inventory.

Everything to be uniform,
Order and incomprehensible
To the people, young and old,
As unthinking and insensible.

Everyone thus obeys
Petty laws of officialdom,
Thus demeaning the spirit,
Stealing rights to freedom.

Jealousies vie with reason,
Yet without common sense
Official uniformity
Is to life, a grave offence.

Fronds of Willow

𝆑eathered fronds of willow
    Hang luxuriant to the ground,
Wind touch'd leaves of yellow
    Fall colourfully gown'd.

Beside the river, meant
    For to satisfy great thirst,
Yet also in gardens green
    Is found, shading the earth.

A tree of spreading beauty
    Softly tranquil to the eye,
Nature's own creation
    Full worthy golden life.

Tell Me Now

Tell me now, what can I do
    To understand the world?
Is it just that I refuse
    As some, to be compelled?

Tell me now, what do you say,
    Do you have an answer?
Why is it, I need to know
    There's such cruel drama?

Tell me now, I need to learn
    Why ignorance abounds?
When some look the other way
    And stupidity confounds.

Tell me now, then, if you can
    Why such evil remains?
I can only understand,
    Humanity's to blame.

Winter Elements

Winter's early morning
    Produced a rush of arctic air,
A myriad passengers
    Of ice-cold flakes, all flurried there.

Mark of the northern winds,
    Severe, the harshness of the clime
That sweeps English meadows
    Bringing frost, snow and ice-rime.

The nights of velvet black
    Inset with burning jewels of fire,
Days see a dim-lit sun,
    As winter elements conspire.

The Tale-Teller

A tale in the telling
    Is as many a tale is told,
And the telling of every tale
    Is, the listener's ear to hold.

Therein lies such art
    As touches in part, romance,
With skill, the teller spins
    The tale, the more to enhance –

Telling of such a tale,
    To weave each word like magic,
Binding all in a spell
    Interwoven with the fabric –

Of a tale-teller's story,
    As he illustrates each moment
With changing pitch and tone,
    Telling of total involvement.

No More Will I Ride the Highway

No more will I ride the highway
    On two wheels of thunder,
Cleaving the air as an arrow,
    Silence, ripped asunder.

Astride the throbbing motor
    Vibration, fumes and speed,
You are part of the machine
    With such urgency and need.

No more will I ride the highway
    In tune with maturity,
Driving four-wheeled vehicles
    In comfort and security.

Behind the roaring motor,
    Information and speed,
You press the accelerator
    With such urgency and need.

Living Marionettes

The very living populace
    Of Great Britain today,
No longer hailed the epitome
    Of tolerance, come what may.

A once proud and noble people
    Have been brought to their knees,
Jealousy and ignoble thoughts
    Make them ill at ease.

They are treated as if dummies,
    Living marionettes,
Are jerked about by their strings
    To dance their pirouettes.

If those in power and office
    Continue to connive,
Marionettes become people
    And people will survive.

By Track and Muddied Lane

Journeys in the country
    During a winter weather's calm,
Shows a bright lowly sun
    Spreading light 'cross field and barn.

The darkened face of earth
    Stares up at a landscaped sky,
As brooding woodlands stand
    Depressingly devoid of life.

The tracks and muddied lanes
    By which the traveller must go,
Are an inspiration
    To lovers of an abstract show –

With ruts, holes and mud
    And dips, as seen on furrowed field,
Leaning forty-five degrees
    Such, to make the traveller yield.

If these dips, ruts and holes
    Mud, cracks and angled tracks and lane
Defines a country drive.
    Then in future I'll think again.

So It Ever Will Be

Thus so it was
    And so it is,
Yet ever will be,
    Exchange and change of life
From one time to the next,
    Continuously see,
As year on year
    Each following on.
Through limitless time,
    Father to father's son
In generations past,
    A never-ending line.
So all life lives
    Within its moment
And within its age.
    Whether past or future
Nothing remains the same,
    Thus, there must be change.

One Step Further

To go one step further,
To listen one moment longer,
To praise one more time,
To help one be stronger,
To help one in need,
To help ponder,
To help,
One.

Mist

Hangs the water vapour
    Thick, deep and wet,
As a veil, to hide all
    Thus, as to protect.

Moisture-laden, heavy,
    Water-hung droplets,
Glistening coats reveal
    Running rivulets.

And seen most eerily
    Such phantom light, clings
To part hidden, shrouded
    Everyday things.

Why Do You Ask?

Why do you ask
These things of me?
Seeking answers
That truly be,
So out of reach
In perplexity,
That even I
Who wish to see,
Complex answers
Though literary,
Uninformed
Philosophy,
Who seek as you do,
Complexity
Strives to define,
Accuracy,
To arrive at
True history
Of which we seek,
Both you and me.

Winter Contrives

The harvest moon has gone
    From September skies,
And the cold light of stars
    From November rise –

Where frost-cold biting air
    From December, lies
Dew-heavy, long and dark,
    While the moans and sighs –

Of bitter lasting winds
    Seeking, without eyes,
Do ply a dance of draughts,
    As winter contrives.

All Is White

The cold rain falls
    And puddles form,
The verge is mud
    And winter's born.

The light grows dim
    And winds turn cold,
The sky is grey
    And frost is bold.

The day is short
    And night is long,
The sun glows red
    And soon is gone.

The trees stand stark
    And snow falls light,
The river's ice
    And all is white.

Gravity

The apple falls,
   Hits the ground,
Plants shoot up
   But soon fall down.
All that's up
   Soon is found,
Falling a'back
   As if unwound.
For all that grows
   Upon the earth,
Static or moves
   Since its birth,
Obeys the law
   Of parity,
Nature's own
   Gravity.

Locomotive

Fire and water
    Coal or wood,
A little oil
    Shows, what could –

With artistry
    Be created,
When steel and iron
    Are mated –

To cunning form,
    Where beauty
And the machine
    Are acutely –

Merged, as one
    Emotive,
Steam-born living
    Locomotive.

Day Progresses

Puddles crackle underfoot,
    And sun reflected
Brilliance from silver
    Ice, blinds the eye.

Painting and carpeting,
    White crystalline frost
Covers the scenery
    And ground, like sugared spice.

The palest of turquoise
    Colours the high
Veil above, where puffs
    Of cloud ride the sky.

While the winter's orb
    Of fire, travels low,
Creating shadows long and dark,
    Day progresses to night.

Among the Crowd
A Christmas Poem

The sound of carols
    Drifting on chill air,
Cold nose and fingers
    That are a-tingle.

Sleighs a-glitter
    Full of presents,
Decorations, parties
    To plan and link-all –

With fat Father –
    Christmas happily
Among the crowd
    With eyes a-twinkle.

The whole wide world
    Is brightly coloured,
As red, green, silver
    And gold all mingle –

With drap'd and hung
    Fairy lights aglow
On trees, while bells
    Merrily jingle.

Burning Flame

Truth may be to some
    An inconvenience,
Laughed at by others
    With indifference.

Scorned by so many
    As beyond their belief,
In their reason, that lies
    Give hidden relief.

Unlike the men of truth
    Who utter no false lie,
But speak both true and straight,
    They would rather die.

For such, are like men
    Who could not take the shame,
They hold their honour bright
    As a burning flame.

The Tree

The tree stands naked,
    Seemingly devoid
        Of present life.

The once-proud growing
    Gown of fresh leaf green
        Now lately lies –

Rust brown and forlorn
    Upon the cold ground
        Brittle and dry.

Yet, life remains still
    Within woody stems
        To again pry –

Each new bud open
    In the springtime suns
        Warming, whereby –

Once again she stands
    Gowned in fresh green,
        To beautify.

A Silver Sun

Over the wide sea,
    Over the high land,
The clouds ride low
    White and bland.

The air is filled
    With water drops,
Hung suspended,
    Obscure dots.

That veil the light
    In ghostly mist,
And pale-lit shrouds
    Floating wisps.

Through this hanging
    Opaque shutter,
Sunlight changes
    In colour.

Rising gold becomes
    Diffused, filter'd,
Transmuted to
    Bright silver.

Due Care

Wild willows used to stand
    Where now leads a road,
And where the village pond lay
    Home to duck and toad,
Stands now a supermarket
    Engulfing the land,
In layers of concrete
    It's so out of hand.

Should they forget to stop
    Regardless of reason,
To build, build and build,
    It could be classed as treason
To land that is your shield,
    Nature being finite
Should have the same due care,
    As they put into the climate!

Clocks

The clock that hangs
    Upon the wall
Or stands upon a shelf,
    As one stands tall,
By name, a grand
    And occupies the hall,
Like village clock
    On church withal
They each do show the hour,
    Both large and small
Throughout each day,
    Our mind, to time recall.

'Tis Not Just the Light

Gold in the morning
    Silver at night,
Sun and moon together
    Do share their light.

'Tis not just the light
    Received from the sun,
We need her glowing rays
    Each day to come.

While the pale-lit moon
    Is romantic,
And reflective in guise,
    Sycophantic.

One sustains with warmth
    For us to live,
As one is mystery,
    A lover's gift.

Rose-Lemon Skies

After the dash and rush
    Of rain against the ground,
Hissing and splashing
    Tattooing of sound.

While thunder, now silent
    Has ceased to hammer,
All that was under
    The clouds' dark banner.

Drifting to distant hills
    The sullen veils depart,
Leaving a mystic light
    In which the skylark –

Rises on high, to clear
    Fresh rose-lemon skies,
A gift left behind
    As summer storms die.

Sundown

In deepest bronze,
    Such a sunlit end
To the short day,
    As the horizon lends
Drama to sky
    And land, in fire,
To complete yet
    A day to inspire,
As many have been
    To poet, writer,
Soldier, sailor,
    Each to make brighter
History or romance,
    With soft colours found,
In golden gloaming's
    Beauty, at sundown.

Forgotten House

The old grey house stands
    Alone, forgotten
By life and history,
    Now partly rotten.

Does it remember days
    Of family laughter,
Children at their games,
    The mistress, the master.

Summertime and picnics,
    Drinks in the garden
At warm party times,
    Polite please and pardon.

Many years have now
    Passed since folk lived here,
The once-proud house, stands
    Forlorn and austere.

The Biggest Game of All

So the politics of the world
    Continue to enthral,
As one side wins or loses
    The biggest game of all.

The game of this one-upmanship
    One man or one party,
Striving to gain the upper hand
    Their rules, good and nasty.

Why are they so bound and beguiled
    By thoughts of wielding power,
Over their fellow men
    When life is but an hour.

So seems the life of men today,
    Why do they strive in vain,
Could they not share, in mind, ideals
    Of enlightenment again.

Dogs

Dogs are, as dogs be,
    In mud and puddles
Some of the time, at
    Others, wanting cuddles.

Yet the dog is true
    And ever playful,
A mucky pup, but
    Yet always faithful.

He yearns to be loved
    And loves in return,
So proud of his master
    You are his concern.

His trust in you is more
    Than you will ever know,
His life for you he'd give.
    A dog, as dogs forgo.

The Days of Old England

The days of old England, are past,
    As the days of Great Britain,
In the hands of selfish souls
    Shall be at best, smitten.

The days of glory and honour
    Belong to her finest hours,
Once mistress of all the seas
    She's been made to cower.

It now beholds the British spirit
    To face anew such weakness,
Give old strength to her again
    Banish this false meekness.

The faults lie with the government
    This year, two thousand and eight,
Belittling the people
    With a control-freak state.

Fiction to Future Days

And should those early
    Writers of science fiction,
Be alive today
    To have conviction.

Their ideas of space
    A half-century ago,
Were on a true path
    The world, theirs to show.

That time, takes real time
    For all true founding precepts
To become working theories,
    Hypothesis and concepts.

And so, such time passed,
    That we see a satellite,
Orbiting station
    And first mega-flights.

This great adventure
    Breed of heroes, who challenge
Stark comprehension
    Of truth, yet manage –

Hardship and danger
    Airlessness, joy and despair,
Hot burning friction
    Speed, as none compare.

Off-world launching pad
    And a vital training base,
For deep space surveys
    And future spaceship days.

Degree By Degree

We are as a race,
    Determined to understand,
Geography and
    History of man.

We learn such lessons,
    School and university
Whet our appetites
    With complexity.

We slowly acquire
    More knowledge of subject,
Thus we acknowledge
    The more, we conject.

We add and inject
    Ev'ry new understanding,
A philosophy,
    Or a moon landing.

We pry and we try,
    Experiment and research,
The more we find out
    The more we must search.

We now see the light
    As human psychology
Unravel secrets
    Of cosmology.

We painfully see
    That the more we understand,
Only brings more questions,
    To further taunt man.

We know we must seek
    Only degree by degree,
Then such mysteries
    Will be ours to see.

Intrigue and Greed

Intrigue by intrigue
    And greed by greed,
Fanatic by fanatic
    By stealth, are agreed.

In selfishness, strike
    Defenceless folk,
Destroying all decency
    As if it's a joke.

Stealing and laughing
    And banking cash,
Faulty politics aid crime,
    Institutions crash.

Intrigue, greed and stealth
    Will be brought down,
When there's nothing left but fear,
    And fear is unbound.

Ignition

The sun ignited
    Millions of years ago,
To give heat, not just
    To itself, but to give show,
Lighting up planets,
    Our earth with her bright warm light,
The solar system
    As the heart and very life.

So is the motor
    Whatever type and engine,
It remains quite dead
    Until spark, with fuel blending,
Switching ignition
    Ignites controlled hot fires,
And the motor becomes
    A breathing machine, alive.

As all too often
    The anger humans inflict,
Builds up to ignite
    A nation in some conflict.
Or perhaps, just two
    People, in argument mood,
Before they can stop
    Ignition, destroys the two.

Foolish Fancies and Otherwise

Everyone has foolish fancies
So don't deny this fact,
It doesn't matter who you are
We all put on an act.

Do you fancy lots of money
Or be a company boss,
Money does not buy happiness
Companies can be lost.

What about an expensive car
Perhaps with a chauffeur,
Imagine the cost of upkeep
Paying for a loafer.

Is it a sultry young woman
Or handsome man t'fancy,
They may just empty your pocket,
Expensive romancing!

Instead of foolish fancies
What is there otherwise?
Get rid of your foolish fancies
They only compromise.

Set your sights on ev'ryday life,
Select what you do best,
What is your greatest ambition?
Apply this, your personal quest.

A Ship of Shadows

There is a story, long since told,
    A tale from ages past,
Of mystery and legend born
    From night-dark shadows cast.

There floats a ship, a darkened ship,
    She rides the northern skies,
And no one knows from whence she comes
    Or goes, or where she plies.

Her hull and masts of shadows made,
    Her sails of white moonlight,
Starlit lanterns a-glinting clear
    Proclaim her part of night.

And of the crew who sail the ship
    Not one have yet been seen,
For faerie-spirit some have said
    Do crew the ship unseen.

She sails the mists of mystery,
    A ship of moonlit shadows,
She rides the northern winter skies
    Beneath the stars, above the snows.

She rides the glowing ghostly clouds
    That fly before the wind,
And race across the moon's lit face
    Like fish on silver fins.

When moonlight fades, and shields her face
    The ship cannot be seen,
Yet travels through the heavens still,
    Unknown, in secrecy.

No sound is heard, no joyous song,
    No merriment is found,
Some say we only see and hear
    What mystery allows.

Her voyage is unknown to all
    And her identity,
Perhaps one night, we may see her,
    With banners flying free.

With hull and masts of shadows made
    And sails of white moonlight,
Riding the northern winter skies
    Amidst a star-set night.

The Printed Word

The printed word has taught man all
    Down the long ages,
From the crudest primitive starts,
    Hieroglyph stages
And mystic Norse-made runic marks,
    To Greek and Latin words
Adding to the mix of sounding
    Tongues, thus confounding
Language as we know it today.
    Even so, many tongues
Survive, to complicate the way
    We try to understand,
And therein lies the malady,
    Though words have taught us all,
It truly is a fallacy,
    Words also, can befool.

In My Mind

How is it I look like this?
    When I don't feel, I look like this,
I feel like I've always felt
    When I didn't look like this!

I used to look young and spry
    Smooth of skin and bright of eye,
Brown hair now has turned to grey
    Now I think that I'm a lie.

In my mind I'm still quite young
    But life I know, has almost run,
I don't recall those passing years
    Rushing my life through rain and sun.

Mind and body, both cause pain
    But which of them, can you blame,
The body, which always ages
    Or the mind, which stays the same.

The Rainbow

Prismatic reflection
    Light-bending curve,
Colouring the sunlight
    As if to serve –

And grace the open sky
    With gifts of colour,
Bright ribbons arching high
    Beyond the thunder –

Clouds, a glowing beacon,
    An amulet,
A token of some strange
    Sorcerer set –

To begin some mystic
    Spell, as storm blasts
Induced lightning, flashes
    From the wizard's staff.

Now in after-storm peace,
    The rainbow shines
But for a short while yet,
    A fading sign.

Meteor

From what dark distance have you come,
    Untold ages, tumbling,
Through the vast cosmos
    Coldest of cold, plunging –

On to some mysterious end,
    Or forever roaming
The unfriendly galactic space,
    Ever onward going.

Or be drawn quite unresisting
    Toward a distant sun,
And in such fearsome furnace heat
    Your travelling is done.

Perhaps you may just chance upon
    The blue-white orb of earth.
And so, caught by her attraction
    To fire and gas revert.

Old Secrets

Hot sands of the desert
    Cold ice at the poles,
And sweat-soaking jungles
    Old secrets could hold.

For buried long ages
    These artefacts lie
Made not of this world
    But with history, tie.

Temples, carv'd with machines,
    All part of man's fate,
Now are identified
    Perhaps a star gate?

One day, all will be clear
    For time will reveal,
Right from the beginning
    Man's future was seal'd.

Christmas Morning

Awake to morning, still in dark
    Excitement overflowing,
This is the day of all year's days
    Christmas morn, is it snowing?

And so, the leap from out of bed
    To stocking or Christmas tree
To see what magic, joyous red
    Mythic father left, to please.

Then to shout or jump with pleasure,
    Sit amidst coloured paper
Wrappings, tinsel, tape and boxes
    Mind and spirit to savour.

Both young and old, it's still the same
    Christmas, creating yearning,
The longed for giving and love,'
    Expressed on this morning.

Between Dawn and Twilight

So short a day
    The hours of daylight,
Between the dawn
    And those of twilight.

For only eight
    In hours to see,
After breakfast
    And before our tea.

As for the rest
    All is winter dark,
'Morn and ev'ning
    Captured, become part –

Of the long, cold,
    Black, wintry night,
Before the dawn
    And after twilight.

True Pie or Fable

Strawberry, gooseberry,
    Blackberry pie,
Skylark with pigeon and
    Wily magpie.

A country delight, all
    In the growing
Of colourful berries,
    And of showing.

Or listen to skylarks
    High in the sky,
Or cooing of pigeon
    And smart magpie.

Which in days gone by, were
    Sought for table,
Each a sumptuous pie, made
    Truth or fable.

A Winter View of an English Village

The winter morn' lays quiet and still,
    And from the winding lane,
Through frost-cold wintry air is seen
    Perfection to retain.

An idyllic country village
    Built low into a dell,
With a partly wooded hillside
    Complementing so well.

Yet, only the tall church spire
    And roofs of thatch are seen,
Above the rising fallow field
    Through misty air, so keen.

An English village nestles there,
    Epitome of peace,
Part of the English countryside,
    A thousand years, at least.

Life

Tell us now, each man and woman
    What is this birth and death?
Millennia after millennia
    Recreating new breath.

What is the meaning for all life?
    Whatever life has grown,
Whether by reason or instinct
    The answer should be known.

Even with man's intelligence
    With his philosophy
Cannot answer why life exists,
    Perhaps it's meant to be.

If it's meant, what is the reason?
    A mix of chemicals
Bombarded by an early sun
    An accidental pool?

If life abounds on many worlds
    As those who know, have said,
Then accidents can't be right
    Untruths then, must be shed.

Cell by cell, divide and divide,
    Although it's a miracle
Divide and then again,
    It's so mechanical.

It's just as if an engineer
    Had drawn the complex plan,
Further, then, made automated
    The growing thus began.

Or is there some mighty secret,
    Bound in the universe,
Where all creation everywhere
    Has an unknown purpose.

To which the likes of us are not
    Now privy, least not yet,
Thus it seems, we need to mature
    Before this knowledge is met.

Nothings Is Carved in Stone

Regardless of ancient carvings
    And notwithstanding time,
As with the old history books
    Such laws and rules confine.

So with the world's great heritage
    Great politics of state,
Composers and artists, tradesmen
    And builders, all to make –

Previous history, translate
    Life as an ongoing
Story, repetitive, yet new
    To the time and growing.

For whatever new thought created,
    Whether law or idea,
Philosophy or politic
    Being false or sincere –

Will never in the highest thinking,
    Be thought carved in stone,
For that is left to creation,
    Ultimate power known.

Old Year, Old Lore

The old year ends amongst
    The chimes, the cheer and the beer,
Music and songs, old and new
    Reverberate through the air.
For some, joy, with gusto,
    Yet others, emotions tear,
And so each year thus ends
    For the new, we must prepare.

Every year the same
    Although the participants change,
Music and games also
    Reflect the latest new craze,
As do clothes and manner
    From cottage up to the grange,
Both high and low do share
    End of the year, party stage.

Why these celebrations?
    What are they really for,
It cannot be that we
    Are glad another year is done.
Ages old, the reason
    This festive party lore,
To chase the dark'n cold, to
    Bring back the warmth of the sun.

Eleven or Even Twenty-Six

How many levels exist
   In real reality?
How many worlds reside
   Unseen, yet very close by?
A nanosecond in time
   And a hair's breadth divide.

I hear there are eleven
   But some say twenty-six,
Different dimensions
   Parallel universes,
Are they identical
   Or in stark contention?

I hope all these dimensions,
   Whether there's eleven
Or even if twenty-six
   Stay in isolation,
Such life complexity,
   We wouldn't know what was which.

A Godlike Style

Let the moon bugs roam
    The surface of that world,
Kicking up moon dust
    With antennae uncurled.
Transmitting the facts
    To an orbiting ship,
Or to the far earth,
    How hot the surface, lit,
How cold, when in shadow
    And how devoid of air,
Death stalks the stranger
    Who becomes unaware,
For this takes people
    Of courage and resolve,
Journeys so unknown
    To take, and problems solve.
To place a robot
    Or man, on so hostile
A planet or moon,
    Demands a Godlike style.

A Single Sunbeam

So thick a blanket
    Clouds the sky,
Over this cold land
    And dark lies –

Above the cities,
    The old towns,
Countryside village
    Fox and hound.

Sees yet the smallest
    Break in cloud,
Perchance a single
    Sunbeam, found.

To pierce the dim veil
    One bright shaft,
One beacon of light,
    Moments cast.

My Country

A country born of classic times
    My country, born of majesty,
A country once so respected
    My country, now a travesty.

A country small, who overcame,
    My country, so adventurous,
A country who explored and built
    My country, so pretentious.

A country who help'd shape the world
    My country, of the inventions,
A country in sore battles, won,
    My country, fed bad intentions.

A country once proud and regal,
    My country, led mindless and lame,
A country sad, forlorn and down,
    My country, betray'd for self-gain.

We, Free Men

We, free men of old England are
    Becoming just a little tired,
Of all the flamboyant words and spin
    That make the government liars.

We, free men of old England are
    Concerned with our country's future,
The government just can't govern
    Betraying the country's culture.

We, free men of old England are
    Becoming fast, more angry,
Why the hell, don't they all resign
    Ere resulting calamity.

We, free men of old England are
    Determined the country won't fall,
Don't they realise history
    Shows, the men of old England, soldiers all.

Children of the Mind

As with all birth in nature found
    In all of earth's creatures,
Sometimes a quick simple affair
    But mostly, pain features.

Although 'tis not quite the same thing,
    Bringing forth a child of mind
Induces a similar pain,
    Yet, a different kind.

For ev'ry music composer
    Or artist of repute,
Writer or poet will tell you
    New work only stands mute –

Until sweat and labour brings forth
    The work in final form,
Presenting children of the mind
    Such, are they, to be born.

Two Cats and a Dog

Two cats and a dog
    Went to sea,
As all did agree
    For to see.

Just how big it was,
    And how far,
From here to there by
    Sun and star.

So they took a boat
    A sail boat,
And sailed to see,
    A-taking note.

In failing winds they
    Mann'd the oars,
Heading still onward
    To far shores.

At last, reaching land
    Called France,
Ate some dinner and
    Had a dance.

Then sailed for home
    Most content,
Dreaming of food, so
    Glad they went.

On their way home, they
    Met some fog,
That didn't stop two cats
    And a dog.

So Short a Time

Life is short, but an hour or so,
    Relatively speaking,
Bearing space and time in mind
    Longevity's meaning.

Based upon existing records
    And our own conscious life,
The spark of mind is extinguished
    As if cut with a knife.

It is so short a living span
    'Twixt knowledge and action,
Through school and university
    And job satisfaction.

For only realisation
    Of this short conscious strife
Could make an indentation,
    In this unknowing fight.

This short-lived hectic survival,
    We refuse to accept
As not our true living span
    'Twas God's own concept.

Earth's Historic Song

When will the earth be able
    Strong enough and ready,
To send her children to space
    Disciplined and steady.

Not just to local planets
    But further to explore,
With ships and engines mighty
    Strength with power, yet more.

For we still lack the vision
    The urge and unity,
To bring all men together,
    Earth's diversity.

Only when the world unites
    Will endeavour be found,
To bring to humanity
    Those secrets, old, profound.

This story starts in space-time
    And through the aeons gone,
To the present day remains
    Earth's own historic song.

The Haunting Song

Faint at first, as from a distance
    Soft enchanting notes drift
Into the mind, like whispered secrets
    Slowly forming, to sift
Through the blanket of the mind
    That falls in sleep or rest,
And from the depths of comfort
    Awake to this caress.

As each sound sinks into meaning
    Feeding the melody's flow,
Filling the mind, half remembered
    The tune, repeats and grows,
Thus the haunting song invades
    The conscious mind in strength,
Forcing a willing acceptance
    Of ghost and memory sent.

Winter Rain

Dark and sombre, the winter's day
    Hangs moodily over the land,
Like a mind in deep sadness
    Troubled by the world at hand.

And in the darken'd sombreness
    The tears run free unceasing
Though newly sprung from the well,
    Spilling and ever increasing.

The rain falls, warmed not by heart,
    Spirit or love and ungodly,
Yet winter clouds in greyness, form
    Thus a tenuous body.

So liken'd to the soul of one
    Who in despair, brings on the tears,
So like the winter rain that falls
    And courses freely year on year.

Quietly She Will Sleep

There is an old island
    Just west of Europe, of fame,
East of the Americas
    And north of the Spanish main.

An island climate told,
    Upon her people and land,
Strength and ingenuity
    With daring, went hand in hand.

Thus was forged a country
    Not unlike the ancient Greeks,
Smallness became greatness
    And so heroes did achieve.

Like the islands of old Greece
    Their glory so long passed,
So, the island of Britannia
    Her history, now cast –

And her future will no longer
    Be emblazoned across the earth,
Yet, quietly she will sleep,
    Awaiting a future birth.

In Brilliant Splendour

Bursting suddenly upon the land
    Light exploded across the garden,
Such a well kept ornamental place
    Where once, one said please and pardon.

Rising higher, obliterating shadows,
    The burning sun in brilliant render
Lit the burnished golden sundial,
    Marking the early hour in splendour
To dance among the plants and pots,
    Each pencil shaft of sunlight, forming
To seek every inch of garden thrust
    So spontaneously into light of morning.

There, the clock upon the tower wall
    Strikes the hour, complementing the sundial
As if to agree this time, on this day,
    In this quiet summer place, pause awhile.

Wimblington Village

Wimblington is a tidy village,
    Not to be confused with Wimbledon
Of international tennis fame.
    Just a village, neither short or long.

Standing upon a gentle rising
    Ground, just south of the Fen town of March,
The village is beginning to grow
    Yet slow, still nestling 'mid birch and larch.

Interspaced with road and twisting lane
    Lay green meadows with pony and horse,
Setting a picture 'twixt old cottage,
    Bungalow and modern golf course.

Not as sleepy as once, years ago
    Nor quite the contemporary life,
Just something in between, neither one
    Or other, a village without strife –

That holds the best of the old and new,
    It suits the folk who live and breath
And play and love in this little space,
    Wimblington, a pleasant place to be.

From Your Doorstep

From your doorstep to the path
    And from the path to the road
Beginning with one small step,
    Is but a short way to go.

For the road when you tread it
    No matter the reason why,
Once you leave your childhood home
    Goes on through the tears and sighs,
Your life is to carry on
    Yet crossroads there, will be shown
And diversions, left and right
    As in marriage, or alone.

All must travel life's old trail
    Which from your doorstep, goes on
Before you, as the years pass
    The road runs still, winding long.

Sentimental Journeys

Sentimental journeys
    Don't mean much anymore,
From childhood homes and young friends
    To old schools, long before
We knew of heartache and youth
    That hurt, as we grew up,
To be what we should, or ought
    To be, yet become stuck
Either in a rut, marriage,
    Or perhaps profession
Dims the past and future sight
    Of memory and vision,
Where once one was so eager
    To return and to find
Those far away days, it seems
    Such pictures in the mind
Grow dim, expectation fades
    Regardless of meaning,
Place, county, holiday gone,
    Other thoughts and feelings
Slowly invidiously
    Pervade your waking mind
Forcing you to accept your life
    However you may find.

Of Meadows Sweet

The green field lays
    Beneath the sun,
Where horses graze
    And hedgerows run,
Along the edge
    Of meadows sweet,
Where buttercups
    Are clustered neat,
The rabbits run
    Their trail by hedge,
Where from the low
    Grows thick the sedge,
Now as the sun
    Pervades the scene,
And warmth cloaks all
    Are busy bees seen,
Then birdsong heard
    From nearby trees,
Sound and vision
    Compete, to please.

Middling, Muddling, Maudlin

Middling, muddling, maudlin,
    The mind in retreat
Or so it seems at times,
    Slow and incomplete,
It is as though the mind
    Has changed a gear,
Slowing the brain right down
    So it would appear.

Nor even did it ask
    To do such a thing,
Middling, muddling, maudlin
    So the brain can't think,
Perhaps some refreshment
    Will help do the trick,
A pick-me-up to start
    Hoping I'm not sick.

A little fresh air now,
    Will that d'you think help,
Is it that I lack sleep?
    I'm to bed at twelve,
I think I know what's wrong
    I've been working hard,
My mind is feeling tired
    So thinking is barred.

Procession

The moon turns round the earth,
    The earth spins on itself
By gravity's possession
    And travels round the sun.

The sun moves through the spaces
    Of the vast galactic wheel –

As the stars turn through procession
    With their astronomical graces.

Confined or dedicated
    Prisoners of laws revealed,

Places for everything
    Everything in their places –

By explosion or compression.

Thoughts on Destructive Construction

Although I love the motor car
    And have driven all my life,
It really has gone too far
    Causing traffic jams and strife.

There are far too many roads
    And therefore too many vehicles,
The railways should take the loads
    To make the roads more cheerful.

It isn't just the cars and roads
    That anger and annoy us,
Laying concrete by the load
    Bricks and mortar building must –

Cover near-all growing land,
    Or so it would certainly seem,
With government protected scams
    Selfishly building on green.

Soon this beautiful landscape
    Will a sprawling metropolis
Become, with stamp-sized parks laid
    And patrolled by mind police.

A One-Time Suburbia

I'd like to take you back now
    To a time far more respected,
Where more freedom was allowed
    And the people seemed contented,
Happier with suburbia
    In themselves or in a crowd.

I'd like to tell, wish to state
    That everything was less hectic,
When folk went to work at eight
    Back home at six by steam or electric,
The private car took some of course
    But the trains were never late.

The restaurant, old English inn
    Were a must for most gentlefolk,
Friday night or weekends, where the gin,
    Whiskey or Martini would evoke
That feeling of well-being, away
    From home, with a touch of exotic sin.

With the Ford Prefect or Morris Eight
    Now tucked up in the garage,
Eight o'clock sharp saw the green baize
    Set for cards and snacks of fromage,
Sunday was the day for gardening,
    Hobbies, or just a lazy day.

(Circa 1930s through 1950s)

Ten Million Sparkling Stars

Sunshine, moonshine, starshine,
    The earth is bathed in photon
Particles, cosmic and gamma rays,
    Plasma winds and violent storms
Rush through space, flooding all
    In an ultraviolet craze.

Each source a raging furnace
    Atomic fires of diverse heat,
Stars of white, blue and red
    Beguile with their aged power,
Only satellites like the moon
    Show light that is reflected.

Ten million sparkling stars
    Ten million nuclear fires,
All competing to light up space
    Ten million starlit years
Of heating their children's children,
    Five billion years of warming each face.

Garden Goblin

There is a secret goblin
    At the bottom of the garden,
He lives in the garden shed
    And keeps the tools all sharpen'd –

At least that's what the gardener said,
    If you leave a pot of honey
He'd clean so spick and span,
    But he'd really like some money.

I've taken him some honey
    And twice a little money,
But I've never seen him working
    Which I think is rather funny.

I've looked inside the shed
    At breakfast and at teatime,
The honey and money were gone
    Of the goblin, there was no sign.

When I talk to him who knows
    About the goblin in the shed,
He just smiles and taps his nose
    I think he's the goblin instead.

Upon a Skyline

When I look upon the skyline
    After sundown 'twixt light and dark,
The line of the horizon shows
    A contrast, where light and shadows mark
The ending of a sun's traverse
    And the beginning of starlight,
Within the deepest blacken'd sky
    Washed by a moon's ghostly white.

When I look upon the skyline
    Thus, conversely, I can see
Between the dawn and end of night
    The line of the horizon gleams,
When contrasting light and shadows mark
    A rising sun's brilliant array,
Bringing a golden dawn to chase
    The nightly denizens away.

A Thunderbird

On a rising wind, faintly
    Like the sound of distant drums,
The beat, beat, beat drifted
    Strongly upon the ear like some
Heavy footed animal,
    Or ponderous beat of wings
Of one giant bird, heavily
    Making its way against strong winds.

Slowly and rhythmically
    The drumming drew much closer,
Clearly now, the sound was heard
    A deadening thudding rotor,
Beating the air to ground in waves,
    The helicopter came into view
Passing overhead and deafening,
    As airwave pressure continued –

To shock and press upon the mind
    With such force as to nullify,
At the time all thinking process
    Until the press was neutralised –

    And the thunderbird had left.

On Wind Power

See the wind farm props on tower
    Slowly turn providing power,
Prevailing wind is there to use
    But not so fierce to blow a fuse.

Helping to cut our bad emissions
    Are those who think it is their mission,
Wind-driven feeble electric
    Powering the humble domestic.

Such a small electric current
    Yet makes each fine view redundant,
It will hardly measure on the grid
    Planting them in rows unbid.

Multiplying, now the towers
    Like giant metal flowers,
Yet what happens when the wind dies
    Unsightly stand, attracting flies.

Nature's Bath Day

Down the lane the rain is flowing
    Down the lane the puddles form,
Running off the wide grass verges
    Running off the garden lawn.

Riverlets racing from each driveway
    Overflowing drain and pathway,
Obliterating edge of roadway
    Turning all into a bath day.

Rain and driveway, verge and lawn
    All converging on the lane,
Add to nature's downpour flow
    But rain itself you cannot blame –

For, it feeds and washes as it goes.
Cool and refreshing English rain.

Nature's Heyday

Down the lane the sun is shining
    Down the lane the sunbeams fall,
Shining on gabled houses
    Shining on the garden wall.

Lancing, dancing, from each window
    Scintillating door and gateway,
Dazzlingly on rippling pond
    Brightly warming to a heyday.

Sun and window, house and wall
    All reflecting on the lane,
Add to nature's sunshine bright –
    Such jewels as summer inflames –

The brilliance in a summer's light.

Nature's Clean Day

Down the lane the wind is blowing
    Down the lane the gusts do bluster,
Coming from the open spaces
    Coming from each gap to fluster.

Driving down each separate sideway
    Growing stronger on path and road,
Battering the plants in gardens
    While dust eddies do swirl and flow.

Wind and sideway, space and path
    All converging on the lane,
And leafy whirlpools fly and scatter
    Before old nature's broom this day.

    Sweeping away dead matter.

Progression To Regression Via TV

The precision of television
    Once a well-timed media,
Newscasts to comedies
    Domestic shows to Aida,
All scheduled to precise timing
    Without the interruptions,
Advertisements and crime scenes
    We never saw corruption.

A cut-glass accent was required
    To be an announcer on TV,
And in our thousands we watched
    Programmes made for us to see,
Yet such, is so-called progress
    Which progresses in reverse,
Where has the accurate timing gone
    Where the polished spoken verse.

Now advertisements, so boring,
    Bad manners and background sounds,
Narration in ill-spoken English
    Compete with expletives, found,
Have we lost our sense of propriety
    Have we lost responsibility,
Have we lost the British spirit
    Have we lost our identity.

    Are our youth to be fated
    Our country contaminated.

From Here to Where?

From here to where?
    That's the question,
Where do we go?
    What suggestion,
We're in a mess
    And no mistake,
The government
    Is just a fake,
Only believes
    In party views,
Cannot see all
    The common truths,
And from all this
    One man believes,
He's the answer
    To the world's griefs,
Even if not
    So serious,
It would of course
    Be contradictious,
Of one who took
    Prime position
Without mandate,
    Opposition
Tries to deal with
    Arrogance and
Those who meekly
    Allow the stand,
Now the country's
    In financial
Dark depression,
    Debt substantial
All part of world's
    Large regression,

Due to bankers
    Greed and selling,
But also due to
    Incompetence,
Of those by whom
    Intolerance –
Of such measures
    Were overlooked,
Undisclosed, not
    Misunderstood,
So here to where?
    The question lays
At all those feet
    That are thus paid,
To guide and run
    This nation,
Not to cheat, fail,
    Use their station
For profit or
    Reward when in
A seat of trust,
    Deception is the sin
By which you will be judged.

Beyond the Yonder

There comes a time within a time
    When we sit and ponder,
What lies beyond the mind's horizon
    What lies beyond the yonder.

No matter the time by date or year
    Wherein wide open space you are,
In darkest deep or within the light
    What world, planet or star.

For all, of sentient spirit
    Yearn to discover unknowns,
Mysteries that lie beyond sight
    Where the wings of mind have flown.

Far away and over the hills
    Across wide oceans and seas,
Beyond the darkest forests
    Mountain range and valley.

Or out towards the distant stars
    Imagination flies ahead,
It is the force that moves us forward
    By curiosity are we led.

The Creator and the Destroyer

Whatever the conceptual theory of time
    Whether dimensional, particle or abstract,
How ever it came into accepted being
    Time has a most destructive act.

With theories of light years and speed
    With one living longer and faster,
If one could ride the photon particles
    A Godlike electromagnetic master.

Even then, upon your returning
    Time would have ravaged all that you knew,
The passage of dimensional space-time
    Destroys all but the hardiest few.

For all matter and all spirit of life
    Their creating and living day by day,
Can never withstand this continuum
    Matter and life grow old and decay.

Time is the enemy of all that is
    How ever long it lives or exists,
Sooner or later it crumbles to dust,
    Explodes or dies or dissolves into mist.

Time is the creator of all that is
    Time is the ageless employer,
Time is the master that none can resist
    Time is the great destroyer.

Fall of Night

I see the lighted lamps
    Gleaming through the trees
At dusk, on an early
    February evening.
The sun's last red streaks
    From the sky, had hidden
Below the darken'd cloud
    That lined the horizon.
The moon had crept brighter
    Into the reaching night sky,
A pale yellow crescent
    That rose silently on high.
So as the shadows fall
    Light and colour faded,
Darkness enveloped all
    And land, the night pervaded.

Winter Elementals

A short time of light
    A white fall of snow,
A little touch of frost
    A cold north wind blow.

Each lays siege in winter
    Each element in being,
Each show their prowess
    Each of them competing.

Such that when combined,
    These elementals wrought
Together such striking
    And fearsome results.

Snow

With snow on way
    To whiten all,
Full faceted
    Water – ice fall
Brings false delights,
    Snow – white,
    Snow – bright,
    Snow – bite,
    Snow – fight,
    Snow – right.
    Snow – flight,
    Snow – height,
    Snow – quite,
    Snow – night,
    Snow – sight,
Yet snow enthrals
    And all above
Could thus befall
    Those whom snow, love.

Particles of Everything

A myriad tiny fragmented
    Particles of everything,
Which go to make up common dust
    Pervades our lives, mostly unseen.

Densely floating in the air, only
    Sunbeams illuminate they're there,
Covering all and in between
    Until the duster shows us where.

Or when the vacuum suction's been
    Sweeping, cleaning, carpet and mat,
Embracing and placing each mote
    Captured inside a bag compact.

Yet living and breathing we are still
    Taking in this great multitude
Of free microscopic matter,
    All molecule by molecule.

The world is full of debris unknown
    But then we should not really care,
For we are part of the very dust
    Around us, all history shares.

The Prize Is Yours

Patriarch to Pharaoh
Priest to Pope.

Chieftain to Crown
    Courtesan to Queen.

Soldier to Statesman.
    Policeman to Politician.

From beginning to end
    Past, present and future,
Position thru' position
    In every culture.

Once, long ago, ideas
    First adopted, became more,
A practice to bemuse
    And not to enlighten, as law.

To hold and continue
    So to govern, or for power,
To command and obey
    From tent up to tower.

To obey is to grow in stature
    In the eyes of those in control,
Conform and do as they say
And **THE PRIZE IS YOURS** to hold.

Impedimenta Regimen-ta

I am a free man my dear sir,
    I live in a democracy!
I therefore obey the law
    Pay my taxes diligently.
        So
Speaking to the corporation's
    Very own planning department,
I required a small extension,
    Sorry, it's not an improvement.
        When
I painted my front door pale blue
    I, received a letter that week,
I'm afraid it's not the right hue
    Paint it as others in the street.
        Then
I just left a bit of rubbish
    In the wrong coloured refuse bin,
They left the bin quite unemptied
    But are suing me for this sin.
        And
The council just won't speak to you
    There's just a mechanical voice,
I just don't know what to do
    For there just isn't any choice.
        But
I know I'm a free man my dear sir,
    I believe in democracy!
But there's such impediment to reason
    Such regimen in law, such hypocrisy.

The Coming of Spring

After the cold, dark rainy days,
    The white of snow that comes
With falling temperatures
    And frost-covered surfaces, sums
Up the British winter so well,
    Yet must come before the advent
Of spring and all the beauty
    That heralds this season, has meant.

The woodland carpet of bluebells
    Anemones and aconites
And yellow garden daffodils
    Alongside pale narcissi
Field and lane, hedges springing
    Into life, bordering hawthorn
Chestnut, poplar, oak and ash,
    Following the early snowdrops' form.

Then as the warmer breezes blow
    Across meadow, town and garden,
Apple blossom shows pink and white
    Along with cherry and almond,
All without regard to world events
    Nature plays her hand to always bring
Inspiration, for our spirit to seek
    Beyond itself, with the coming of spring.

Time and the Hour

Tick-tock, tick-tock, tick-tock
    The hours slip by as always,
From this o'clock to that o'clock
    And the second hand obeys
As it sweeps around non-stop,
    While the striking chime proclaims
The hour, the pendulum cares not,
    But swings through its vertical plane,
    As is its lot.

    For time and the hour
        Is ecumenical,
    The clock has no power
        It's just mechanical.

Rabbits All

Young rabbit, small rabbit,
    Large rabbit, old,
Out in fields of snow
    Out in the fields so cold.

Hard to run. Hard to hop
    Ice, unfeeling feet,
Looking, searching for
    Any food that we can eat.

The nights are long and damp
    Days are for seeking,
But snow lays deep
    And less, are we feeding.

If we survive to last
    Into spring's bright sun,
Then we still may die
    By the shooter's gun.

Universe of One

If, for us, such
    Time and distance,
Measures untold
    Or circumstance,
Cannot unfold
    To show us how,
Or when, or why
    The past, is now.
Such reasoning
    Is so beyond
The intellect,
    That pursues long
Argumentative
    Theorems of time.
Space distortions
    The Möbius line,
Of hypothetical
    Theories of all
Matter and life.
    Irrefutable
Evidence does
    Not, in the light
Of human knowledge,
    Exist for insight
To acknowledge,
    Untold distance
And time, becomes
    For instance,
A universe of one.

The Eternal Habitat

High above our heads, unseen,
    High above the chimney pots,
Above the many rooftops
    And the varied green treetops,

Up into the very heights
    Beyond that which can compare,
Further than the wispy clouds
    Passed the thinnest of thin air,

To the edge of coldest cold
    On until beyond the earth,
The nether region of space
    There you'll find mysteries' birth.

High above, yet on all sides
    And downwards from where you are,
The eternal habitat
    Of each planet, sun and star.

And surely there are neighbours
    Who one day will come to call,
Let's pray, we may be able
    With forethought, have new concord.

A Blue Chevrolet

Blue as a high-summer sky
    Yet with a subtle difference,
A touch of blue-lilac hue
    Or lavender's pale variance.

However you look at it
    By whatever light or shade,
It's a most appealing colour
    That ever a car was made.

By geometric line as well
    The contours are so graceful,
It is, I think, most elegant
    And the seats so comfortable.

She's smooth as well as stable
    This Lacetti, a Chevrolet,
And not at all expensive
    As most prices are today.

She's not such a sporty car
    As most would say or think,
But now, I know different,
    Because she goes like stink!

An English Lane

And does the English lane
    Still exist,
To meander to where
    One would wish,
To see and hear summer's
    Beauty 'midst,
The fields and meadows near,
    Of birdsong
And sight of fallow deer,
    Plough'd furlong,
The dark running hedge
    Of hawthorn.

Pink and white of wild rose
    Haw and hip,
With the sloe of blackthorn
    T'gether sit,
Bordering the wayside
    Leading to,
An English cottage quaint,
    Of straw roof,
With its two guarding geese
    Apple tree
And cat upon the porch,
    As English
Country lanes should be.

The Colour of Light

Sunlight weakens from purest gold
    Through orange to deepest red,
As it nears the horizon
    When another day has sped.

While the copper face of the moon
    Begins to rise into the darkening sky,
Changing to a creamy yellow
    Then brightest white, when on high.

A shining sight complements all,
    The stars, as the bluest diamonds,
Sparkle amidst the backdrop
    Of black velvet, like fire gems.

Here and there the fast streak
    Of burning flame, as a meteor
Bores through the high atmosphere,
    An incandescent visitor.

And thus the lamps of the world
    Light all our days and nights as seen,
By day to plan, do and build,
    At night, to rest, love and dream.

Dracula's Daughter

Long legged spider
   Sitting in the corner,
      One leg on the web
         Quickly to warn her.

Many eyes a-watching
   From its hideaway,
      Waiting a visitor
         To touch the web array.

Patiently she waits
   Still and quiet and dark,
      Hidden by the shadows
         Hungry, like a shark.

Suddenly she pounces
   As her web vibrates,
      Stunning her tiny prey
         For her thirst to slake.

Long legged spider
   Sitting in the corner,
      Retreats back to wait
         Like Dracula's daughter.

Life Extraordinaire

Wherever you look, life teems,
    A million species or more,
Not including bacteria
    Or microcosm's microbe store,
Nor single cellular life forms
    All of which are uncountable,
Yet life above these levels
    Is just as formidable.

In their myriad forms diverse,
    Was it natural selection,
Or did the gods have a plan
    That caused sophistication,
Of insects, beasts, fowl and fish,
    Were they all for mankind's use
And made for him to accomplish
    His rule, even to earth abuse –

Or just victims of nature.
    That I believe the latter
For all that would be worth,
    Yet, belief is all that matters.

Thus, life matters and must come first.

Rest the Pen?

Like so many others
        With quill or brush or pen,
Over so many years
        Whether women or men,
Must, therefore, beware a time
        When you believe the last
Of lines is finally writ,
        Your views, themes or verse cast
With humour, anger or wit
        Into the lap of the gods,
Awaiting fate from the world's
        Critics and critique, at odds
With others of diverse view,
        To complete the writer's lot.
When all the artist wanted
        Was to hand a newborn plot
To others, undaunted,
        As the writer's ambition
The need to create, is a force
        Obeyed, until completion.
Until such time arrives
        When the years and the hand send
A message, the other way,
        Perhaps it's time to rest the pen?

        Or does the pen have more to say?

BOOK II

PRESENTED LIGHT POETRY

By

Elizabeth Stanley-Mallett

CONTENTS
Book II – 2008

Autumn Jewels	131
Winter Sun	132
Dawn	133
Dreams of Home	134
It Is All Wrong	135
Mars	136
Furry Companion	137
Guiding Star	138
To Win	139
Heatwave	140
Narrow Byway	141
I'm with You	142
The River	143
Jupiter	144
Full Circle	145
Saturn	146
Music	147
The Poet	148
Imagination	149
Time Control	150
Storm	151
The Village	152
Just Pages From a Book	153
Does Life Go On?	154
How Is It?	155
My Family	156
Friends	157
Food	158
Nature's World	159
Snowfall	160
Complacency	161
War	162
A Blank Canvas	163
The Beginning of Space-Time and Man	164
Life's Patterns	165
Be Candid	166
Shadows	167

Whispers	168
Little Bun'	169
Our Team of Two	170

Autumn Jewels

As autumn bites again a year
   Escorted by the breeze.
Colours are painted everywhere
   Palleting the leaves.

Gold, scarlet, crimson and red,
   Yellows chasing brown.
Swirling, whirling from the trees,
   The leaves come floating down.

The gossamer-fine spiderwebs
   With cartwheels grace the lawn.
As frozen glinting drops of dew
   Create the scene at dawn.

Riding with the morning mists
   On rising clouds of haze,
The air is chill with hints of frost
   In the shorter autumn days.

Orchard boughs are weighted down
   As harvest fruits mature.
Autumn reveals nature's jewels
   To crown another year.

Winter Sun

Summer's reign has gone,
    The sun is low in the sky.
November comes along
    With bonfires and a guy.

Weaken'd warmth on field
    Winter wheat, now sprouting green.
Tractors haul sugar beet yield
    As trees grow stark and lean.

Flowing full and high
    The river dark, fast running.
Moorhens timid, shy,
    Retreating, ever shunning.

Birds hunt hips and haws
    Storing fat for cold to come,
Mobbed by greedy jackdaws
    Snatching each precious crumb.

Crimson, now the ray
    Dips lazy in the west.
Loath to leave, the weary day
    Is forced at last to rest.

Dawn

The world is asleep in pseudo death,
    Roused at dawn by morning breath.
Stirrings in velvet canopy of space,
    Bringing fresh life to every face.

Dreamers emerge from their cosy womb,
    The veil of night gives up its gloom.
Stars fade, surrendering to day
    The moon swings low in sunlit ray.

The rolling mists run out of steam,
    Dissolving gently in the beam.
Dewdrops cling to blades of grass
    Loath for interlude to pass.

The bat returns to his musty church,
    Night owl slumbers on dusty perch.
This is the time dark turns to light,
    Power of day breaks power of night.

Dreams of Home

The distant hills reflect my dreams
   So near and yet so far.
I wish I was thistledown
   To float to where you are.

To soar aloft and over the hills
   On wings of summer's song.
The fragrant breeze blows straight and true
   To home where I belong.

My wounded heart's in torpid state
   To wait time's healing hands.
My body moves, a robotic shell,
   But no one understands.

The pain is cruel, it's there for life,
   I try to fight despair.
I pray the night will quickly pass
   'Til the day that I'll be there.

It Is All Wrong

The world in its path rolled along
   'Til one event harboured wrong
Causing such changes to start
   Tearing nature's rhythm apart.

Dragged simple man in tow
   Broke his spirit forced to bow
For them, as gods of fear and might
   Made him work, made him fight.

To mine for them, plunder the earth
   Slaves created, flawed at birth.
To dig and delve the precious gold
   Distant ailing home uphold.

These same gods made many mistakes
   Human slaves made many escapes.
Man evolved, in spite of them
   And given time, false gods condemn.

Mars

Mars, the glowing ember in the night,
   Cast by Jupiter, to smoulder alone.
Grim Lucifer, waiting to ignite
   Your anger by storm and war full blown.

Drums of war throb out their angry beat,
   Linking up hate, envy and greed
Man to fight man, in utter defeat
   His planet ravaged, anarchy freed.

Your legions of death marched straight to Rome,
   Standards aloft "Ares, Odin" they hoard
On seven hills they camp, now they are home
   Your day has come as they kneel to their Lord.

Lord of destruction, leper of space,
   Great avenger serpent of old
The harvest is in, at end of the race
   Your kingdom void, a cinder of cold.

So you wait again for a millennium or two,
   Brooding alone, hiding your pain
Another young orb comes in view
   Havoc will spread and chaos shall reign.

Furry Companion

Upon my lap all soft and warm,
    Razor claws against my knee.
Trusting me to do no harm,
    All in peace and harmony.

For many years he's been my friend,
    Contact and company, close.
Dreaming through the day, content,
    Lost in languid repose.

He seems to sense when I am down,
    And snuggles closer with a purr,
Looking at me with blue eyes, round.
    A bundle of soft white fur.

When he comes in from the night,
    Leaves and twigs attached to him.
His coat bedraggled, no longer white,
    Begging for food, making a din.

In the garden he leaps up high,
    Running and tumbling over the ground.
Trying to catch a butterfly,
    So amusing, such fun to have around.

Guiding Star

Venus, planet of emerald hue,
Brightest jewel in heaven's stance.
Morning and evening star in view,
To what do you owe your brilliance?

Were you the star guiding the magi?
Protecting the bare stable,
Shining, beacon in the sky.
Guarding the new one's cradle.

Venus, goddess of beauty and love.
Heavenly name and gleaming sphere.
Cousin of earth, portent above
For this king we must revere.

On shrouded vaporous world,
Mystical globe, features unseen.
A servant, destined to unfurl
His banner to flutter supreme.

And from your turbulent shrouded face,
Projects a spirit and the light
Creating a lord of grace
Born to exceed Olympus in height.

To Win

Alone, drifting along
    Nowhere to go or see,
Life had turned all wrong
    Leaving a wreck of me.

Nobody there to hear
    Controlled by another,
Tried to please, left in tears,
    Foremost I'm a mother.

Time took toll, cut me down
    To make me look so small,
Sinking, almost to drown,
    Full laughing at my fall.

Recovering, to start again
    Trying to heal and mend,
Giving strength to sustain,
    To win and comprehend.

Heatwave

It's summer now, the sun is high,
    And soil craves moisture from the sky.
Creatures seeking shadows, to fend
    Off heat until day's end.

The red deer forages the dried up glen
    Parched grass fails to comfort him.
Lean, his frame, nourishment is scant
    Seeking shade for a needed pant.

The eagle shuns the noonday glare,
    Too hot to chase the mountain hare.
The moor ignites, and burns dark brown
    The grouse inspects the hardened ground.

A mirage lures tired pilgrims on,
    Water's there, but now it's gone.
A trick of light a kind of dream
    Nothing's real, nor what it seems.

In this arid, dry and dusty land
    The stream is mud, the meadow sand.
Let rain cascade upon the plain
    And bring green life to earth again.

A Narrow Byway

The road to ruin is a wide highway,
    Like lemmings, we rush to die.
The road to success, a narrow byway
    Halt now and contemplate why.

Super highways let us speed past
    All that's beautiful and bright.
Slow down, pause, look around you,
    Nothing is only just black and white.

Life's journey can be fast or slow
    The choice is yours for panic or calm
Helping others, or turning away
    Planting seeds of peace or harm.

The next generation will judge
    Do we leave gardens or waste.
Sparkling streams or rivers of filth
    To preserve or tear down in haste.

I'm with You

I'm with you in the sunbeams
    Dancing on verdant plain,
I'm with you in deepest dreams
    Learning to live again.

I'm with you in meadow flowers
    In roses kissed with dew,
I sense you in April showers,
    My rainbow shining through.

I'm with you in thunderstorms
    In the force of driving rain.
As gentle droplets form
    To bless the earth again.

I'm with you, as down the lane
    Each primrose so abides,
As, fragrant, small and gay
    In woodland border hides.

I'm with you beside the river
    Flowing gently from its source
Riding on wavelets, ever
    Nearer a homeward course.

The River

The river flows its mysterious course
    Deep, dark and unknown.
Snaking its way through verdant banks
    Reflections in silver shown.

On one foot the heron waits
    An angler standing still.
Lightning strike, for hunger sates
    With this fish, in his bill.

Along the banks gnarled willows grow
    Leaning far into the stream.
Bowing supple branches low
    In flowing homage scene.

Chugging boats go by for pleasure,
    Down the watery way.
Lounging occupants taking leisure
    On this summer's day.

The river's argent band, nurtures the life
    Of fish in the shallows.
Food is there, more to entice
    Shaded still, by green willows.

Jupiter

Jupiter, king of the planets,
    Great lord of the sky.
Magnet of the solar system,
    The all-seeing eye.

The great red spot whirls for ever
    Creating mighty storms.
Poisonous, hostile weather,
    Giant, in gaseous form.

In name a roman god,
    Zeus, an omnipotent Greek.
Ruling with an iron rod
    Capturing strong and weak.

Collector of space debris,
    Of destructive, awesome knocks
Defending earth from entry
    Of deadly, killer rocks.

Full Circle

The morning of life is fresh and new
    Like paw prints trailing through the dew.
The vibrant feel of each new day
    And honeyed scent of new-mown hay.

Blackbirds shrilling their harsh alarms
    Waking lover from a lover's arms.
To greet the day with hopes or fears
    Euphoric smiles or salty tears.

Then struggling through each latter day.
    How to live and how to pray.
With passing seasons youth has gone
    The body fades, the soul holds on.

As evening falls so quiet and still
    The spirit's free to soar at will.
From this older life's grief and pain.
    Phoenix-like will rise again.

Saturn

Saturn, lord of the rings,
    Mystic vision to share,
Alluring planet in all the system,
    None other can compare.

Embracing many moons,
    Huge Titan, is but one,
In rings, ten thousand more,
    Reflect the distant sun.

Champion of old age,
    Maturity and wisdom
Changing, with new learning
    From fool into old sage.

Fear not time of faded glory,
    When rings cease to spin,
Millennia will pass,
    For time has no meaning.

Music

Music is a delight to hear,
    Soothing all distress away
Taken slowly, a pleasure,
    A pure art for the ear.

Transports the spirits high
    Emotional and strong,
Moving even stony hearts
    So tears come to the eye.

Melody enthrals,
    Orchestral or solo,
Harmonious tapestry,
    Music, enchanting all.

Creating scenes of love or war,
    Conjuring history,
In colourful sound
    As in days before.

The Poet

The poet aims to strike a chord
    To touch the reader's heart,
Bringing to life, words by verse
    In the wordsmith's art.

To embrace the reader's mind
    With impressions true,
By seeking for the truth
    He achieves anew.

The poet links mind to past
    And touches now and hence,
Daring to hope his work
    Brings forth love, joy or sense.

The poet lifts emotion
    From the factory floor,
Projecting the images
    Boldly to the fore.

Imagination

Imagination takes the mind
    Into a magical world
Of faerie folk and kin
    Fantastically unfurled.

High the spirit soars
    Over woods, hills and dale,
In dreams of fond prosperity
    Illusions prevail.

Imagination holds the soul
    In emotion's desire,
Colours everything in sight
    Setting the heart on fire.

Taking away restraints
    Of everyday life,
Imagination takes over
    Erotically to rise.

Imagination is wondrous
    Activity and ideas
Leaving pain and hardship
    Behind, as distant fears.

Time Control

Tick-tock, the ticking
    Echoes from up high,
Sounding rather quick
    As time gallops by.

Too fast to appreciate
    Rushing life style
Speeding through the years,
    No time to wait awhile.

Loudly resonant
    Striking the hours,
Setting precise order
    From ancient clock towers.

All disciplines rely
    On correct time sight,
What if it all went wrong
    Stopped during the night.

Chaos would take over
    Alarms would cease to ring,
Grinding all to a halt,
    Soon, unrest to bring.

Storm

As lightning strikes the steeple
And clouds clash together,
Stair rods spear the ground,
Noisy, stormy weather.

Huddled in their rooms
Children quake in fright,
Storms lash outside
Lasting all the night.

As if to never end
This long downpour wild,
Flattening the gardens
Landscapes defiled.

Rain in sheets flood the roads
Rivers swollen and high,
Burst their banks and overflow
Boundaries now defy.

Cattle huddled in fields
Seek the higher land,
Cold, wet, hungry, they
Fail to understand.

Come the morning, the land
Mirrors a reflected flow,
Of splendid bands of colour
From a sky-born bow.

The Village

A tiny dot on the map
    Fertile land, outlying farm,
Clustered, rustic cottages
    Quintessential charm.

Standing in the blacksmith's shop
    Far too close to forge,
Hampering the busy smith
    The idiot, called George.

Once it had a village store
    Bright Aladdin's cave,
Selling necessary goods
    Food and so much more.

The church high upon the hill
    Master of the scene,
Dwarfing everything in sight
    That's built around the green.

Serving all the country folk
    As sails go whizzing round,
The miller turns the local wheat
    To flour, rough and brown.

Horses drink from the village pond
    Where frogs congregate to spawn,
Cartwheels soak, to swell the wood,
    And field mice in the corn.

Just Pages from a Book

Textbooks generally show
    History as dull and grey,
No urge to read and learn
    Of kings and queens to know.

History tells the stories
    Of folk, down the ages,
Illustrates, in legend
    Past defeats and glories.

Crusaders royal and lowly,
    Battles fought in far-off lands
Striving hard to liberate
    Old Jerusalem, the holy.

Back at home, the tyrant John
    Taxed the peasants hard,
Grasping food and seedcorn
    Until it was gone.

Hidden in the greenwood
    Protected well by Herne,
A ragtail band of outlaws
    Lead by Robin Hood.

They roasted deer in forest deep
    And took from greedy rich,
To aid sick, poor and needy,
    Their secrets long, to keep.

Does Life Go On?

This life, but a stepping stone
    Wedged between two portals,
Could it be there's a door
    To show we are immortal.

Through to another plane
    Or to a higher level,
If you do as be done by,
    Heed not any evil.

We could pass to many levels
    Or dimensions close by made,
Is there a right path
    To ascension laid.

Live each day as best you can
    When the right time comes,
Another light will reveal
    You free of earthly bonds.

'Tis simple to take those steps
    So life goes on its way,
Death comes, as a catalyst
    Perhaps a brighter day.

How Is It?

How is it that I first saw you
   In my dreams so long ago?
How is it arms hugging you
   Were really mine as now?

Were you my one and only
   My reason to rise each day?
The man I've always wanted
   The one for whom I craved?

How is it I have found you
   After looking all my life?
How is it I had determined
   That one day I'd be your wife?

There's no doubt I fiercely love you,
   As once again I'll find
You are more than a memory
   Living within my mind.

Were you out there looking
   Trying to seek for me?
Search my heart and you will see
   My love, for all eternity.

My Family

'Tis not a comedy show
    For them, such strong feelings,
They amuse, hurt and charm me
    Always tug at heartstrings.

Strapping sons, fathers proud
    One left to join the pool,
Of parents with youngsters bright
    Learning much from their school.

One such child, young lady student
    Echoes Grandmother's wish,
She studies in animal care
    To fill a veterinary niche.

Sons have Mum's business head
    One outstrips the rest,
His acumen and judgement keen
    Proves he's from the best.

Friends

Few friends stand fast and stay
    When times are dire and grim,
When help is wanted badly
    Most skulk and slink away.

Not many linger and give a hand
    Of support and fellowship,
Very few take your part
    Or try to understand.

This world is swayed by greed
    Avarice dominates the many,
Friends learn to render alms
    Cries for help they heed.

A true friend there, come what may
    A staunch prop to provide,
Comforting and supplying
    Strength to fight each day.

The true friend is a treasure
    Not to be treated lightly,
Valued and long preserved
    Gold, without measure.

Life has youth and maturity
    Friends can make it pleasant,
Forming strong bonds, that can
    Last into perpetuity.

Food

Is it a pleasure or curse
    The love of food so fine,
All tastes are sweet or sour
    Long life or hasty hearse.

Food can energy provide
    Stoking the inner man,
To perform mighty feats
    Boosting ego and pride.

Juicy fruit picked in prime
    Ripened in golden sun,
Tease the palettes fair
    With variety sublime.

High praise on our lips
    The humble potato earns a place
A staple food that many chose
    To simply serve as chips.

Heaped banquet table groans
    As rich and favoured dine,
Filled with gas they cannot move
    Can only lie and moan.

Cheese, made large and small
    Blue, strong and mild,
Young or fully matured
    So ripe, the maggots crawl.

Fish, meat, fowl, protein, more
    Hard work for the jaw,
Bits between our teeth and
    Pickings, there galore.

Nature's World

Diverse, large and very small
　The world of nature falls,
Jungle beasts to arctic voles
　Wonderful species, enthral.

'Tis magic how the worker bee
　Finds her way back to hive
Laden down with pollen for
　The queen to make royal jelly.

Like speed of pneumatic drill
　Woodpecker raps a tree
Selected, so only he can
　Customise, at will.

Epitome of mother love
　Polar bear in icy cave,
Giving birth while waiting
　'Til snow thaws above.

A butterfly on jungle leaf
　Basks in tropical glare
Too long will scorch him dry
　Shadows bring relief.

Near-blind bats at dusk
　Catching moths on the wing
Using radar to guide their path
　A miracle of trust.

How do salmon leap upstream
　Hard against the flow
Instinct pushes them to breed
　Their ancient, silver, sheen.

Snowfall

The snow fall overnight
    Blended verge and road in one
A cotton wool, silent mask
    Reflected in moonlight.

Proudly, against the sky
    A lone pine stands aloof.
A silent sentinel
    To a hound's distant cry.

Settling, soft, flake on flake
    Chimneys frosted on the top,
Delicately icing all,
    As a Christmas cake.

Hopping, midst the cold white land
    A robin hunts for food,
Nothing there, but in the house
    A banquet grand.

Complacency

Why sit and let it happen
    Stupid laws and tax too high,
Ears are deaf and eyes closed
    Why is fight and grit lacking?

Complacency, creeping foe
    Invidiously gaining foothold,
Until life is sour and futile
    And we're trapped, the last blow.

But, don't let the uncaring
    Ruin our cherished land,
Make a stand, take charge
    Show courage and daring.

England, was a pleasant country
    Now destroyed, brought low,
Only honest men can,
    Change this complacency.´

War

Nothing can be more futile
    Nothing is ever achieved,
Religion usually starts it
    By misguided beliefs.

Civil war is by far the worst
    Making friend fight friend
Pointless horror and slaughter
    From beginning to end.

Terrible conflicts have taken place
    False gods are venerated,
Massacre, followed by famine
    Barren land, there generated.

There is no sense in conflicts
    Fight not their evil wars,
Life, far too short to waste
    On a murderous, worthless cause.

A Blank Canvas

Where are the words I feel,
Mind seems blank, nothing flows,
Lots to say, but it's just a
Blank canvas with no appeal.

From childhood days to teen years
Feelings grew and fast outpaced
Purse, knowledge and home life,
Strength ignored the jeers.

Work obtained, revealed high hope
Showing ways to forge ahead,
New friends made, comfortable life
Marriage, promised lots of scope.

The canvas, now coloured in
Assorted scenes depicted there,
Words have come, finally, to
Vindicate, tenacity wins.

My canvas, no longer blank
Now painted by life's course,
A blend of belief and drive
A rebel of neglected ranks.

The Beginning of Space-Time and Man

In the beginning there were gasses
    Spinning in vastness of space,
Rotating for untold aeons
    Forming, coalescing, masses.

Making planets, moons and stars
    Thousands coming into being,
And orbiting one hot sun
    A watery orb, close to mars.

Giving life to temperate spheres
    Earth, being only one,
Many supporting green plant life,
    Evolving, man appears.

Progressing over millions of years
    Man developing weapons,
Fighting for territories vast
    At behest of pompous peers.

Warring tribes, fearing chiefs
    Fought each other silly,
Ravaging fertile lands
    In deluded beliefs.

Why fight and kill each other
    There really is no point,
Every soldier killed in war
    Leaves a grieving mother.

Why not try this day to ban
    Or engage no more in battle,
Creation is for the living
    Destruction helps no man.

Life's Patterns

I feel compelled to write
    To try and express in rhyme,
Feelings, buried deep too long
    Emotions, free and unconfined.

I feel my task is simple
    Illustrate and entertain,
To educate in poetic verse
    All life's colourful refrain.

Thus, life takes many turns
    Some bright, some very drear,
Through it all shines the gold
    The love of one held dear.

The appreciation of wisdom
    Can only come with age,
Philosophy broadens outlook
    Illuminates life's page.

Life goes on come what may
    Disaster will not block,
Newborn aspirations following
    As aftermath of shock.

Be Candid

Speak the truth, speak your mind
    Do not hurt or pain,
Being candid does not mean
    You have to be unkind.

Opinion can be very direct
    To the point and swift,
Give a little thought
    Your image to project.

Other people may not see
    What you try to say.
They may feel pain and suffer
    So phrase another way.

Let others see you as a friend
    Who utters only facts,
With genuine urge to aid
    Relationships to mend.

By intrinsic, candid word
    Values are transmitted,
Showing you really care
    And wish only to be heard.

Shadows

Images following their host
    Flat creations of light,
From here to who knows where
    Reality or just ghost.

Soundless, silent to the ear
    Shielded from solar glare,
Welcomed as shade by some
    To others, manifests of fear.

Shadow of moon on sun
    Moving over the orb,
Eclipse, darkness on earth
    Until the course is run.

Illusions of the mind
    Shadows worry many,
Past thoughts, fears, only
    Memories left behind.

Did it move or is it still?
    The answer is well known,
Shadows merely block the light
    You see what you will.

Whispers

Semi-muted voices drifting on the wind
    Coded messages, to be passed
Accurately, no chance at all
    Alas, much too late to rescind.

A little prattle, title-tattle
    Malicious seeds taking root
In fertile soil, snowballing on
    Cages, pandemic to rattle.

Secrets, passed from ear to ear
    Instruction to waiting troops,
Important orders to proceed
    If only they were clear.

Whispers should be passed with care
    Think how to transmit,
Good news to cheer, boost morale
    Unvarnished, simple and fair.

Quiet as a whisper is the rule
    Loud enough to be received,
Distortion frequently happens,
    Whispers can so easily fool.

Little Bun'

I'm just a little bun'
    Hopping on the ground,
Chewing up the shoots
    Eating is such fun.

I'm just a little bun'
    I thump when a-feared,
When something's not right
    I run and I run.

I'm just a little bun'
    Foes I have plenty,
Trying to catch hold of me
    But I am only one.

I'm just a little bun'
    One of many that abound,
We must learn to avoid
    All humans when they come.

I'm just a little bun'
    I have an urge to dig
Under the garden fence
    And nibble in the sun.

Our Team of Two

Two together is the norm
    My husband true, and I,
We've queried aspects of life
    To find the reasons why.

The love of my honest man
    Is worth all the gold in mines,
Our team of two will overcome
    All problems that we find.

We pull together our team of two
    Side by side, day by day,
Expressing words and ideas
    In our individual way.

Our team of two match each other
    Perfectly we display,
Harmony in thought and deed
    At our work and play.

Our team of two laugh a lot
    Amusement easy to find,
Funny chat and discourse apt
    Tension leaves behind.

A team of two ploughs the field
    One horse will not do,
On my own I can't succeed
    My husband, I need you.

Our team of two has projects new
    That we will keep alive,
With love and trust we soldier on
    Together we'll survive.